The Wealth Singula

How to use Accelerating Technolog

Table of Contents

INTRODUCTION

"In other periods of depression, it has always been possible to see some things which were solid and upon which you could base hope, but as I look about, I now see nothing to give ground to hope—nothing of man."

As we write this, the economic challenges that descended on the world in 2008 continue to linger. It's easy to share the sense of hopelessness that the opening quote explores. It's easy to share the bleak sense of the future that this quote portrays. The media is full of similar views.

There is only one small challenge. This quote isn't about the present condition at all! Calvin Coolidge said this back in 1931.

Coolidge, standing among the ravages of the great economic collapse, saw "nothing to give ground to hope."

But Coolidge was wrong. By 1931, technological marvels were making their way from the theoretical minds of people like Albert Einstein, Niels Bohr, and Max Planck. These minds, and the minds of other scientists and technologists, would introduce the marvels of innovations, like the transistor, television, lasers, and atomic energy.

The economy, though it took time and effort, recovered and soared to heights that Coolidge could have never imagined.

In the Wealth Singularity, we will take a contrarian point of view from many people who can't seem to see any ground of hope in the current economic conditions. We believe the world is on the verge of an amazing transformation.

It's important to note that Depression is more than a description of the price movements of the stock and commodities market. It's also an apt description of the collective mindset of the era. People lost their optimism and vision for the future. This collective depression only made the recovery period longer and more difficult.

As the country entered World War II, it seemed Americans would never touch the economic good times of the 1920s. Ironically, the challenges of World War II reinvigorated the innovative fires and produced technological marvels that found peace time uses. Transistors, radar, jet power, and atomic energy were a few of the inventions that created the wave of economic prosperity of the 50s and 60s.

In the middle 1970s, it seemed like the bad times were here to stay. War, an energy crisis, and foreign competition staggered the economy. But, less than a decade later, the software and, soon, Internet age ushered in new wealth.

This isn't meant to diminish the pain felt by people during those times, but this pattern is not coincidental. Economist Joseph

Schumpeter called these periods "creative destruction." Old technologies are laid waste by new more powerful and efficient technologies and wealth-building methods.

Look at some of the businesses that have risen out of the ashes of troubling economic times:

- Procter and Gamble (Panic of 1837)
- IBM (The Long Depression of the late 19th century)
- General Electric (Panic of 1873)
- General Motors (Panic of 1907)
- United Technologies (the Great Depression)
- Hewlett-Packard (the Great Depression)
- FedEx (Energy crisis of 1973)
- Microsoft (The 1970s recession)

There's no reason to believe that the current economic climate will not produce similar technological leaders and innovations. In fact, the next wave of technologies are far more powerful and have the potential to be more pervasive than any created in the past.

The idea that ever-increasing technological gains will produce increasing prosperity is central to a group of futurists who say that society is heading toward the Singularity.

The Singularity is Near. So is Unlimited Wealth.

The Singularity refers to a theoretical point in time when technology becomes so ubiquitous and the ability to use this technology becomes so powerful that the universe gets saturated with intelligence.

Several experts say that this technological Singularity is inevitable. The path can be read like tea leaves in the exponential gain of computing power brilliantly exposed in Moore's Law.

One variation of Moore's law states that computing power doubles every two years, while the cost of computing decreases. Proof of Moore's Law can be seen by comparing the size of laptops and the cell phones with their predecessors, as well as the number and power of applications we find on these devices.

We've never seen an increase in intelligence or an information revolution that hasn't boosted economies and personal wealth. After all, technology is nothing more than intelligence in replicated action.

History is full of examples of the wealth-building effect that new technology has on the economy before:

Telephone
Telephonic equipment linked the world in ways that people never thought would be possible. It

also created increases in productivity and germinated an interlinked national economy. (The telemarketer also came into being--you can't have everything.)

Railroad
New steam and diesel technology paved the path for the railroad. Railroads transported raw materials and finished products around the country quicker and more inexpensively.

Automobile
Not since the invention of the wheel has a revolution changed the world as completely as the internal combustion engine. The car created several industries--from car manufacturing to fueling stations to a thriving tourism industry.

Of course, the television and Internet waves brought on incredible boosts to the economy.

Information technology, nanotechnology, biotechnology, integrated Internet technologies, and artificial intelligence may make these initial waves of economic change seem like ripples in an ocean. If the small innovations of the past can dramatically the economy, imagine what these pending waves of technology will do. It will be an economic tsunami.

This exponential explosion of information is starting now.

- More than 3,000 books are published daily.
- There will be more than 1.5 exabytes of new information produced this year.
- New technical information is doubling every two years.

Imagine:

- You'll live longer.
- You'll live better, too.
- You'll use energy from sources you never thought possible.
- You'll tap into your own brain power and unleash the power of artificial intelligence.
- You'll explore virtual reality.

And, you'll have access to sources of wealth that were once unimaginable. According to technology experts and futurists, it's just beginning. Ray Kurzweil, inventor and futurist, believes we will enter an age of exponential wealth generation.

Given that the (literally) short sighted linear intuitive view represents the ubiquitous outlook, the common wisdom in economic expectations are dramatically understated. Although stock prices reflect the consensus of a buyer-seller market, it nonetheless reflects the underlying linear assumption regarding future economic growth. But the law of accelerating returns clearly implies that the growth rate will continue to grow exponentially because the rate of progress will continue to accelerate. Although (weakening) recessionary cycles will continue to cause immediate growth rates to fluctuate, the underlying rate of growth will continue to double approximately every decade.

If Moore's law reveals the exponential growth of technology, then a new law must be named to describe the exponential growth of wealth as the world moves closer to the Wealth Singularity and the inevitable growth of wealth strides along with technology. It's a law we call the "More and Moore" law.

In fact, this Wealth Singularity is already happening.

According to the book Quantum Investing, by Stephen Waite, the initial stages of the Wealth Singularity occurred in the 20th century. More wealth was created in the 20th century than in all centuries combined. The goods and services produced in the 20th century in the United States went from $500 billion in 1900 to $9 trillion in 1990.

Even with the current state of the global economy, investment growth has been no less than miraculous over the century. (Even the dreaded dips of the Great Depression in the 1930s and the deep economic drop of the late 2000s are nothing more than blips on this constant march to the Wealth Singularity.)

And the wealth-building powers will continue to accelerate.

This growth doesn't even account for the most transformative technology that is preparing to sweep us into the Wealth Singularity. These technologies, according to Quantum investing, include:

- Molecular and quantum computing
- Nanomaterials
- Robotics
- Bioengineering

And these are the "expected" innovations. Unexpected innovations are often the real drivers of economic transformation.

There is still more evidence that the waves of the Singularity are lapping on the shores of the financial world.

High Frequency Trading (HFT) is one piece of evidence, albeit a controversial one. HFT uses artificial intelligence and high-speed computers to access markets (called dark pools) before other traders who are using less powerful technology can. These HFT groups take advantage of price inconsistencies, which traders have done for years, but do so faster and smarter than ever before. In milliseconds, these traders can amass millions of dollars.

H-Plus Magazine, which follows Singularity developments, believes this is a revolution. A troubling one, yes, but it's still a revolution.

"Regardless of the debate over how HFT is used in market trading, it's clear that supercomputers can already "outrun and outsmart" individual investors. This isn't quite the Singularity envisioned by Good and Vinge, but it raises some perplexing questions about the use of artificial intelligence to gain market advantage when individual humans 'with slide rules' cannot compete."

-- *H Plus Magazine*

It's important to note, as Kurzweil points out, that technology usually starts out under the domain of the wealthy. But eventually it will become ubiquitous.

"Technologies start out affordable only by the wealthy, but at this stage, they actually don't work very well. At the next stage, they're merely expensive, and work a bit better. Then they work quite well and are inexpensive. Ultimately, they're almost free."

--Singularity.com

The evidence is overwhelming. The Wealth Singularity has begun. The real question, then, is, can you position yourself to take advantage of the Wealth Singularity? Are there ways to use technology to build and manage wealth? Are there technologies being developed that will allow self-directed investors, not just dark pool money managers and hedge fund managers, fast and smart access to financial markets.

We think the answer is yes.

Or, as Kurzweil says, "Ultimately, everyone will have great wealth at their disposal."

In fact, some of the first tools to create this great wealth are already available to you. These tools, when used correctly, can produce wealth automatically, repeatedly, and easily.

In the Wealth Singularity, we'll delve into the archives of the Online Investing AI blog, which discusses new wealth trends and unconventional ways to financial freedom, and introduce you to how you can master the technology of the coming Wealth Singularity.

You'll learn how to make money, save money, invest money, and spend money in this new age of Wealth accumulation. You'll learn some of the wealth-building strategies that are working right now and position yourself for new sources of prosperity.

In this book, we'll share with you a ton of resources that will help you on this journey. And, if you want to read an outstanding book about the Singularity from the titan in the field, get The Singularity is Near by Ray Kurzweil. It's a great book because it is easy to understand and fascinating to think about the ramifications of Kurzweil's ideas. The book that you are reading right now has sprouted from seeds planted by Kurzweil's wonderful book.

Welcome to the Wealth Singularity.

How to use this Book

This book can improve your life, if you allow it. Yet changing and improving requires more than just reading. We want you to comprehend the ideas that we are sharing with you on a deeper level. Therefore, we have added activities at the end of each chapter.

The benefit of each activity is that it allows you to process the information presented. Please do these activities! They will help you get more out of the book. Learning is not a passive activity. To really understand something we need to interact.

Therefore, we have added a place for you to write down your responses to the activities. To print out the interactive activity pages, simply go to the page that you wish to print and choose print from your PDF reader software. Then, choose "Current Page" to only print the page that you are viewing. This will print only that page, so that you do not need to print the whole book. We suggest that you print up the interactive activity pages and save them in a notebook.

Or, if you wish, you can write the answers in your journal. It doesn't matter how you do the activities. The important part is to do them! Taking a first step to achieving your goals is magical, no matter how small that first step is.

MAKING MONEY

The idea that pain and money are linked together is ancient. We earn our livelihood by the sweat of our brows, as the verse goes.

Workers put their "time" in and received a gold watch to signify the most valuable asset that they sacrificed--time.

The business paradigm has changed as well. In the olden days (20th century), people would start a business such as a restaurant or retail store. If they were really ambitious, they would build a factory and manufacture a physical product. Other people struck out on their own selling their expertise (such as accounting) and working as independent contractors.

These entire lines of business have become much less desirable and less feasible due to accelerating technology. Why invest $100,000 in a restaurant that has a 95% chance of failing within the first year? Why build a factory when you have the product manufactured for you for lower cost and no up front investment? Why would you waste your time delivering your expertise when you turn the expertise into an eBook or online service, and deliver it to an unlimited number of clients using none of your time?

The critical distinction in the above examples is *leverage*. Leverage is what wealthy people use to make large amounts of money using little of their time and energy on an ongoing basis. It may take significant effort to build the business, product or service, but the incremental cost to deliver another unit of the service is very low.

As Robert Kiyosaki, author of the Rich Dad, Poor Dad series, said "We go to school to learn to work hard for money. I write books and create products that teach people how to have money work hard for them."

Accelerating technology (and specifically the Internet) has given massive leverage to everyone with access to a computer. Entire businesses that have the potential to make more money than a restaurant can be set up with hundreds of dollars, instead of $100,000. Leverage provides individuals with the ability to build large successful businesses with little resources.

Changing technology has provided massive leverage. Yet it has not provided the seed to our financial success. Everything in this world (including businesses) starts with an idea. The light bulb was a ridiculous idea. The flying machine was an unproven and stupid idea. These ideas are the genesis of new products, services and businesses.

As the Wealth Singularity dawns, you will make money on what you create, not what you make. In the past, the amount of time and hard work that went into a product was a large part of the item's final cost.

Now, that cost is shrinking, but the price of creativity becomes a larger part. Think about the iPod. Any number of hundreds of devices could do the same thing. The materials and work are about the same to create an iPod-like device. But people are drawn to the iPod . because of its aesthetics and operations. And it's brand!

How will this translate into making wealth for you?

The free enterprise system, powered by ever-increasing technology, is creating more opportunities to create wealth in some unconventional ways. You don't have to be an engineer or product designer, either.

Now, these aren't necessarily effortless ways to earn money, but once set up, they can produce pretty much labor-free money.

Sometimes, when you're doing what you love, it may seem like you're doing nothing. Fortunately, technology has given individuals access like never before to markets and tools.

Interactive Activity: Finding Leverage

1. How has technology created leverage to improve your life?

_____

_____

_____

2. What examples of leverage can you thing of that benefit businesses today?

_____

_____

_____

3. If you were to start a business, what leverage would you use?

_____

_____

_____

4. If you were to invest, how would you leverage technology?

_____

_____

_____

Blogging

A blog (short for web log) is nothing more than keeping an online diary. Only a few traditional diarists have successfully made money from their private thoughts and observations, but thousands of people are earning life-changing sums of money from their blogs.

You can earn money from blogs in many ways.

To prove it's possible, the blogger who is behind Living Off Dividends shows several methods for earning bucks from writing what you want – from everything from affiliate programs to text ads.

Here's how he makes money on his blog:

Here's my breakdown for the 2nd quarter. I made $7,353.84 in online income I made between April 2009 through June 2009. For comparison, I made **$6,760.85 in online income** during the 1st quarter.

- Ebay Publisher Network: $2729.85
- TLA: $1487.09
- Linkworth: $664.82
- Adsense: $382.79
- Kontera: $26.88
- Direct Ads: $1,599.15
- RevResponse: $18.9
- A top Internet affiliate: $79.22
- Other/Affiliate: $244.82

On average, I made just over $2,250 a month.

As you can see, the potential to make actual money from a blog is possible.

But blogging isn't the only way to make money with your writing skills.

Six Steps To Create A Money-Making Blog

1. Find a niche

A lot of people think that blogging is all about finding a cool name and to start writing. That's not what they experts say.

Your first step to creating a blog is to find a niche that you have some expertise in and that interests you.

A niche might be Fantasy Football. But you want to drill deeper. Fantasy Football players with multiple accounts might be closer. Fantasy Football players who have multiple accounts and serve as commissioners of multiple leagues is even closer.

So, what if you find a subject that can be monetized and you have some expertise in, but you aren't interested in the subject?

Avoid it. If you don't enjoy the subject, you're not likely to complete Steps 2 and 3: Produce quality content and produce it consistently.

2. Produce Quality Content

If you blog about something you like--and you're an expert at it--you'll be able to produce quality content. And that will attract readers.

These readers will appreciate your expertise and consider your recommendations for products.

They'll also return for more information. That's why you have produce quality content consistently.

3. Produce quality content consistently

There's no perfect answer to the question: "How much should I blog?" Though, it is arguably the most frequently asked question by would-be bloggers.

The truth is some famous, money-earning bloggers blog several times a day. Some blog once a day. Some blog once a week. And some only blog once a month!

But, it's a good idea to set up a publishing schedule. At least initially--or until you're a famous blogger with readers waiting on every word you transmit--create a regular release of posts and stick to it. Readers will expect it and check back frequently. It also builds up your writing discipline.

4. Promote

You can promote your blog (in a non-sketchy way) by adding links to your post on Twitter and your Facebook account. You might also want to add it to social bookmarking sites, like Digg, Reddit, and other sites that directly address your subject area. (For instance, personal finance bloggers can add links to Tip'd, a social bookmarking site for financial matters.)

5. Comment

Here's one idea that many bloggers overlook.

Don't look at your fellow bloggers as competitors. They're actually collaborators. When you have an appropriate comment, don't be shy about adding a comment to a forum post or blog post. Don't add extra links in the body of your comment or post. You can usually link back to your site by adding your blog URL in the name field.

6. Monetize

Find affiliate and advertising partners for your blog. Or, use your blog to attract clients.

Interactive Activity: How can I make money by Blogging?

1. If you were to start a blog, what could it be about?

_____

_____

_____

2. What interests do you have that you can turn into a popular blog?

_____

_____

_____

3. What expertise or experience do you have that you can share with other people?

_____

_____

_____

4. What problems have you searched for that could make a great blog?

_____

_____

_____

5. What is special about you that is interesting? Do you have an interesting job (like news reporter, fighter pilot or tightrope walker)?

_____

_____

_____

6. What is interesting about your environment? Do you live in a place that is interesting, like Hollywood, Paris or Tokyo)?

_____

_____

_____

Writing for Online Sites

Blogging is just one way to leverage your writing skill to make money during the Wealth Singularity.

If you like to write, you can add your own content for sites online sites.

You can also build your own microsites and pages on big-named portals. These sites then give you a share of the advertising revenue.

Two of the biggest are eHow and Squidoo. You can also earn revenue by writing how-to articles for HubPages and Demand Studio.

Video is becoming increasingly popular and will continue to do so as we draw closer to the Singularity. If you're a video entrepreneur, there's sites for that, too.

Besides writing for online sites, try writing a book. Thanks to technology, it's never been easier.

Imagine if you wrote 200 articles that earned a dollar a day through revenue share. That would build up $73,000 a year in residual income.

Digital Products and eBooks

You can write and produce your own eBooks and digital products (like video and iPod seminars). You can also sell the stuff that other people created by becoming an affiliate.

Some of this material can be re-purposed from your blog or web site.

Check out eJunkie and Clickbank for ways to do sell your eBooks and digital products. It's a great way to sell information and expertise.

One of our favorite resources for making money online is Cloud Living. It is the story of a guy named Glen who was barely out of his teens when he began to discover how to earn wealth and maintain your freedom. He walked away from a lucrative development career to indulge of his dream of living the life he wanted. We're lucky enough that Glen is sharing this secret.

In the eBook Cloud Living, Glen passes on how he generates a 5-figure monthly income online and built a blog with 4,000 subscribers in less than one year. We really love this book because it provides clear and actionable information about how to succeed at making money online.

Another opportunity exists with the book you are reading right now. Does this book make sense to you? Are you getting value from it? Do you think that other people would find this book useful? We have an affiliate program for people who want to earn money by selling this book. Visit Online Investing AI for more information.

Selling Information and Expertise

A rather new form of book-selling, the eBook is usually offered in pdf form.

Most think that offering digital products to readers is an insignificant royalty stream. You won't make the New York Times bestseller list, right? You might not make the bestseller list, according to books like the 4-Hour Work Week and Career Renegade, writing electronic books or producing electronic products can deliver a regular stream of residual income.

Jonathan Fields, who wrote Career Renegade, points out several successful projects that created residual income for their authors in his book. Leo Babauta's Zen Habits (zenhabits.net) sold thousands of copies and, with no publisher and agent to divide up its earnings, each sale was pretty much all profit.

So, what do you need to know about creating residual income with information products?

- **Find a niche.**
  Just like starting a good blog, you need to pick a subject that you like and write a book or produce a video that fills a need in that niche.
- **Start a blog or "platform".**
  You want to build a relationship with your readers so they know and trust you.

27

- **Become an authority.**
  Build trust in your community as someone who knows a lot–or someone who can connect them with sources who know a lot.
- **Sell or attract.**
  A digital product can be sold, or it can be a vehicle for future communication with your reader.

Now, let's look at some of the pros and cons:

- **Pros**
  The great thing about eBooks and other digital products is that when you sell them, it's pretty much all profit.
- **Cons**
  You need to build an audience, which can take time. The other drawback, you'll have to do the work. You have to write, for instance, and some people don't like to write.

Here are some resources to help you get started:

- Copyblogger's great article about creating eBooks that sell.
- Lulu.com (publishes eBooks)
- Clickbank (sells eBooks and creates affiliates for your eBooks)
- eJunkie (another great place to sell digital content)
- Your Portable Empire by Pat O'Bryan
- Made to Stick by Chip and Dan Heath

Make Money Selling Real Books

Print-on-Demand Publishing is another baby step toward the Singularity. It allows unpublished authors to create, print, and distribute their books much like real publishing houses do. It's called Print on Demand publishing.

In the olden times, the big challenge of writing a book was in finding a publisher. People would stress about how to get their book published, and send it to dozens of companies hoping that one would be kind enough to publish their book. How times have changed.

Now, getting a publisher is simply another method of distribution, and it's not necessary to find a publisher to create a book. Print-on-Demand publishing allows anyone to print and distribute their own book for a minimal cost (about $50, at this time). They no longer need the help and attention of another company to make it happen.

That does not mean that having a traditional publisher is a bad thing. Arguably, it has many advantages, including increased visibility and distribution. The problem is that the vast majority of books never get enough attention to become well know. Print-on-Demand technology as well as other information distribution advances has reduced this barrier.

Self-publishing with print on demand technology gives you the opportunity to write, publish, market, and sell your traditional book.

Lulu and CreateSpace are great places to start for this.

CreateSpace can give you access to their huge online marketplace instantly. iUniverse, owned by Barnes and Noble, offers access to the online market and the potential to sell in the company's sprawling chain of stores, too.

Selling Books and Products

If you like to write books, you probably like to read. And you might have dozens of books lying around. The online market gives you the ability to instantly create your own used book store.

By hooking up with online book sellers, you can sell used books, for example.

But why stop there? By selling on eBay, your product selection can go beyond books and is nearly endless.

Artists

"The future belongs to a very different kind of people with a very different kind of mind--creators and empathizers, pattern recognizers, and meaning makers. These people--artists, inventors, designers storytellers, caregivers, consolers, big picture thinkers--will now reap society's richest rewards and share its greatest joys."

-- Daniel H. Pink
A Whole New Mind

During the Wealth Singularity it won't be what you make... it will be what you *create*... that generates wealth.

Replication machines--think of them as three-dimensional copying machines--are already making appearances in prototyping and fabrication factories. Eventually, they'll be in every household. Manufacturing will be obsolete.

But creating and inventing will never be obsolete. Neither will art. In fact, you can catch this wave on the web right now. If you're an artist, consider selling your works on Etsy (www.etsy.com). And, Ponoko (www.ponoko.com) lets you buy and sell designs and products.

Invention Royalties

Are you an inventor or an idea person?

Creating a product and earning royalties off of it is perhaps the easiest (at least after you sell the idea) way to earn money.

You can use online sources to help build that product, or help sell the idea to industry.

Make sure you talk to someone who isn't a scam artist. Kim Babjak's site (www.kimbabjak.com) is a good place to start to learn about royalties and licensing.

Here's another great site to pitch your ideas: Edison Nation (www.edisonnation.com).

Affiliate Sales

Maybe you don't want to actually sell products.

Another way to earn money is to tell traffic on your website how great products are somewhere else. It's called affiliate sales and a number of professional affiliates make thousands, tens of thousands, and more with the business model.

Here's how it works. Suppose you read a book that you really enjoy, and you think other people would enjoy it. You can sign up as an affiliate at an online store that sells books. They call it an associates program. Then, you can link to the book you just read from your blog, and people can buy the book from the online store by clicking on the link in your post.

Every time someone clicks on the link and buys the book, you get paid! Currently the commission rates are between 4% and 10%. It may not be a large amount of money for each book, but it does provide massive leverage. Once the link is on your blog, it requires no work on your part to make money. And, millions of people can use your link to buy the book!

One affiliate sales strategy is to start a web site about a subject you like and then host ads on your site. If you have a blog, write about these products or offer recommendations. If you have an email newsletter, pass on your recommendations and include your affiliate link.

To get started, visit the sites of products you use and look for a link to their affiliate program, if they have one. You can also join Commission Junction (www.cj.com).

Warning: The easiest way to lose your authority is by passing on recommendations that you don't like, don't use, or, worse, it's a scam.

We firmly believe in the strategies that we share with you. In fact, we use many of them in our site, blog, and even in this book. Many of the links in this book are actually affiliate links. Therefore, not only do we endorse some of the products and services that we link to, we also receive a commission when people purchase them after reading this book.

Become a Teacher or a Coach

If you have special skills, teach them through video chats or on your own membership site.

A membership site is a premium section of your web site that members must pay to access. Typically, it requires a monthly fee. These members can then access your video seminars, post questions for you, read in-depth articles, and other exclusive material.

You can also couple this with other revenue streams, like an eBook. Or, you can use the eBook to pass on some information, but leaves them wanting more.

Teaching will be revolutionized in the near future. Instead of creating compounds to confine children and calling them schools, children (and adults) will learn everything that they need to learn at home. Online videos, training, activities and workshops will make it possible to learn at the pace of each child and at the convenience of their own home and schedule.

Teachers will be able to clone themselves and teach an unlimited number of children simultaneous through new technologies such as streaming video and virtual classrooms. Their experience will improve because they will no longer serve as wardens to obnoxious students. And student's experience will be outstanding because they will learn about all of their interests in a way that works for them.

Education will expand from something that we inflict on our children to something that we want to do throughout out lives. As adults become thirsty for new skills and ideas, online learning will be a natural way for them to acquire new ways of making money or careers. Learning will become something enjoyable and fulfilling that adults will do throughout their lives and at the comfort and convenience of their own home.

Advertising and Web Publishing

Allowing advertising on your blog or web site is another form of residual income.

Online advertising networks and pay-per-click ads have made web advertising easier than ever. By generating interest and traffic to your site, you can convert a number of those readers into customers for your advertisers.

Like everything, web advertising has its own lingo. Here are a few terms to remember about web advertising:

- **CPM**
  This stands for "cost per thousand." (M is the Roman Numeral for Thousand.) The number tells you how much money the ad makes for ever thousand visitors.

- **CPA**

  Cost per Action, or how much you'll make if your reader takes a certain action.

- **CPC**

  Cost per Click. How much you'll earn each time an ad on your site is clicked.

You can read more about CPM, CPA and CPC this in this article from Portal Feeder Pro.

Social Media: Twitter and Facebook

We won't go into detail about how to use social media to make money online. That is a quickly evolving subject that requires specific and up-to-date information. This information is available in abundance on the Internet. If you are interested in making money quickly and efficiently, we do recommend becoming proficient with social media.

The important thing about social media is that it provides massive leverage. It allows an individual to share their ideas and connect to thousands of others quickly and without any cost. Since it allows people to connect so easily, Facebook has become the second most popular site on the Internet!

Social media is another example of accelerating technology (specifically Internet technology) creating massive benefits for billions of people. At the same time, the cost to use this technology is zero. So, that means that we get all of the benefits of connectivity without any direct cost.

Learning Activity: Making your First Blog Post

Are you a little nervous about how to start that first blog post?

Here's a step by step process that will help you brainstorm and organize that post. You don't need to format each post this way, but it helps to have a format for those first articles and when you need some clarity for those moments of cluttered inspiration.

1. Blog Name

Believe it or not, your first step actually starts before you post.

You'll want to come up with a name for your blog. A good blog name is memorable and easily searchable. If you have a catchy name that isn't search-friendly, you can still make a go at your blog. It's just a little more difficult.

Write the name of your blog here:

_____

2. Post Headline:

Think of a few catchy words or a sentence that sums up your post idea.

Write the headline here:

_____

3. Main point:

What's the post's *big idea*? Work this in to your lead or first paragraph. Can you come up with a story that illustrates this theme?

Write the main point here:

_____

_____

_____

4. Sub points:

Add supporting points here:

_____

_____

_____

5. Search terms:

How will readers find your blog or post? Insert these terms into your headline and throughout the post. Make sure, however, that it doesn't alter the meaning of your post. Write for people, not a search engine. List some search terms here:

_____

_____

6. Resources:

Add links that will help your reader explore the subject of your post in depth List them here:

_____

_____

_____

7. Call to action:

Ask for comments or click to your site, whatever your goal is for your blog. Write your call to action:

_____

_____

8. Art:

Check our sites like Creative Commons for access to free art to illustrate your post. Save some good images to your computer so you can use them later. Write down where you saved them or notes about the images:

_____

_____

_____

Creating a Sales Funnel

The more you learn about the Wealth Singularity, the more you'll realize that since information is the most valuable product, every piece of information can be monetized.

Smart info-preneurs create a sales funnel. A sales funnel is simply fulfilling the needs of your customer as they journey along your information path by delivering appropriate products and services. Those products can include eBooks and audio clips, as well as services like websites and membership portals.

Here's how you can make your sales funnel:

- What's your wisdom? Consider the information or expertise that you have. Create a list of those skills, experiences, knowledge, and hobbies.
- What information can you deliver based on that wisdom that will improve the lives, or solve the problems of your customers
- Create Books and eBooks
- Tape a digital lecture and make a digital audio file
- Write a blog
- Hold a teleconference
- Create a membership site

One of the benefits of this technological revolution is that it is very easy to see what other successful people are doing. Why go through all the work of figuring everything out by yourself? It is much easier, faster and smarter to simply model what other successful people have done. Here are some big successes that give us great ideas about how to succeed at making money online.

Success Case 1: John Chow, Mega Money-Making Blogger

John Chow was interested in the Internet, but struggled to make money out of it.

Until he discovered blogging, Chow worked at a print shop. But he later decided the real potential for money rested in the Internet. A pioneer in the new field of Internet money-making, called (at that time) weblogs, later shortened to blogs, Chow began to build his online empire.

His zany approach to blogging gained popularity. Chow was also one of the first to make money--a lot of money--from blogging. His monthly income has zoomed to over $40,000.

You can check out Chow's approach to blogging at John Chow dot Com (www.johnchow.com).

Success Case 2: How Timothy Sykes Makes $80,000 a Month

Timothy Sykes, who we'll mention again in the investment section of the Wealth Singularity, is also a successful blogger. Wildly successful. His blog attracts millions of visitors and brings in thousands of dollars a month income. Sykes has wisely created a sales funnel. Here's an excerpt from his blog about his success at income generation.

> Oh yes, this is an all-time high for me, blowing away my previous record of $70,000 in August 2008.
>
> Read the notes below it and see how they compare to September's $53,000 month, another $50k in October and November's $66k….oh yes, trend followers can see my business is growinggggggg:
>
> December 2008: $83,358
> $20,229 TIMalerts
> $27,688 Instructional DVDs
> $29,407 Advertising & Affiliates
> $2,084 An American Hedge Fund
> $3,950 Trading Profits

Success Case 3: A Zen Approach to Information Products

Making money with online technologies can still reflect your higher philosophies and ideals. Consider Zen Habits (zenhabits.net), an eBook about how to use the philosophy of Zen to improve our lives. It sounds very esoteric and unpopular, but his blog and eBook are huge hits. He makes more than a full time income

45

from these unlikely ideas.

Leo Babauta was a writer who lived on the far-away island of Guam. (In the past, publishers had to live in big cities, like New York City and London. In Wealth Singularity age, you can live in the middle of the Pacific.) Babauta was a writer with an interest in productivity and Zen simplicity. He called it Zen Habits (zenhabits.net).

He began to blog about those subjects and message resonated. Soon, thousands--and then tens of thousands--of people were reading his posts.

As he wrote, Babauta realized that an eBook containing some of the wisdom and tips he collected in his blog would be handy for readers. He created an eBook, Zen To Done, and sold it on his blog.

Within the first month, he sold more than 1,000 copies.

The book currently sells for $9.50. At this price, the book would have pulled in more than $90,500 revenue.

Interactive Activity: You have the info, now what's the action?

1. If you can choose only one topic to blog about, what would it be?

   _____

2. How much money would you like to make from your blog per month?

   _____

3. What are the benefits of having your own money-making blog? List 5 benefits below:

   1.
   _____

   2.
   _____

   3.
   _____

   4.
   _____

   5.
   _____

SAVING MONEY

Technology can help you make money. We've established that.

But now you have access to the unprecedented power of technology to solve the other side of the personal finance equation: saving and spending money. Here are a few ways:

First, the Internet and shop bots can help you locate the best deals. You can also print out coupons and add Internet coupons to your online purchases.

A relatively new e-business allows you to shop and earn rewards. To participate, you join one of the reward sites on the web. Using a reward site helps you save in a couple ways.

First, you get a rebate for shopping. Before you shop, you navigate to your rewards site, which is a portal to web stores. You click on the ad for a product or a store. When you buy a product, you should get a portion of that sale kicked back to you.

The amount of rebate varies, but it's typically in the 10-20 percent range.

But here's another way to save. Rewards sites help limit impulse web buys. You have to think about what your buying and where your buying it. Then you go to the portal and set up your purchase.

These customer-loyalty programs include:

- My Points (www.mypoints.com)
- Big Crumbs (www.bigcrumbs.com)
- Bond Rewards (www.bondrewards.com)
- Blastoff Network (www.blastoffnetwork.com)

Technology is Making Personal Finance Easy

Personal finance is a drag for most people. They hate numbers and have a hard time figuring out how to manage their money. They aren't interested in accounting, and the last thing that they want to do is think about their financial situation.

Managing our finances deals with a lot of numbers and that takes lot of time. And there are so many better things to do in life. At least that how it was before the Wealth Singularity.

With new online tools and more powerful computing technology becoming increasingly prevalent, personal finance is becoming quicker and easier to manage.

It's obvious that computers are good at dealing with boring tasks like adding numbers and generating reports. But even the old personal finances software was quite a bit of trouble to use. The new generation of online tools are designed to be super easy to use, and require no software maintenance on your part.

In this section, we'll show you the tools that can make your personal finance easier. Here are some great sites that you can use to make it happen.

- Wesabe (www.wesabe.com)
  It's not just a community and advice center, the site features tools to help you manage your money. This site has been described as "If Chuck Norris were a personal finance tool, he'd be Wesabe."

- Mint.com
  Mint.com, which was just bought by Intuit, is one of the pioneers in creating online tools for personal finance.

- Geezo.com
  This site's tag line is "personal finance for everyone.

- Buxfer (www.buxfer.com)
  Buxfer is described like this: "Beyond a clean interface for tracking your purchases, payments and trends in your spending habits, the company has been developing some impressive new features."

Other Ways to Save Money:

I haven't met anyone who got rich by skipping Starbucks, but maybe I will in 50 years after their $3 a day has compounded into $1 million. Here's some ideas that can help us save larger amounts of money.

1. Instead of buying a new car, buy a reliable used car (Honda or Toyota) that is 1 - 3 years old. That will save $10,000 - $15,000 right off the bat, and makes it easier to pay cash. It's hard to think of anything better than avoiding debt and interest payments.

2. Turn off the cable or satellite and sell the TVs. Most people spend $50 - $100 per month on TV service, and 8 hours a day watching it. That is $1,200 per year and 3,000 hours. This money can be used to invest or pay off debt.

3. Don't use credit cards *unless there is no other way to pay*. Pay for everything with cash. Ever notice how when we use a credit card, we don't feel like we are spending money? When we use a credit card, on average we spend 30% more than when we use cash. So just by taking the credit cards out of our wallet we can cut our expenses in a big way.

4. Replace spending habits with money creation and learning habits. Our culture is all about consumption: more cars,

more food, more iPods and bigger televisions. The net result is unprecedented spending, increased debt and surging waistlines. When you have the urge to spend money and consume, do something that actually makes money or help you. If you need inspiration, choose any idea from this book!

5. Replace credit cards with check cards. What's the difference? A check card works just like a Visa card, but instead of going on a credit account, the money is simply debited from your checking account. They work everywhere a credit card works. (Contrary to popular opinion, it is possible to survive in this country without having a credit card.) The main benefit of a check card is that it makes us responsible for what we buy, and we see the money taken out of our account immediately.

6. Sell stuff on eBay. Recently I got rid of a bunch of stuff that was sitting around my room that I really didn't want. I like a certain large bookseller (that I can't name) because the prices are much higher than on eBay. The caveat is that it takes longer, but who cares? It's great to get rid of the stuff and make money, even if it takes a few weeks or months.

7. Stop expensive habits cold. We only miss things that we enjoyed recently. After going without something that we

love, we adapt and tend to forget about it. Going out to expensive restaurants is a good example.

8. Don't buy anything on credit. Buying everything with the money we have makes us responsible for what we buy. This will eliminate the purchase of all the stuff that we think we need (like iPhones), but we really don't.

9. Delete unnecessary insurance. Recently a family member had a car accident. She had "30 days of rental car coverage" as part of her auto insurance policy. It turns out that this coverage is a complete scam. Firstly, it only pays if you are at fault. Secondly, it only pays for 30 days if it takes that long to settle your claim. They only pay for 3 days after your claim is settled. That means that if it takes a week to settle your claim, they only pay for the rental car for 10 days. This insurance is completely useless because the chance of using it is incredibly small, and the amount of money they pay (a few hundred dollars) is not worth the premium we pay for the coverage. This kind of insurance scam can be found throughout the industry. Take a look at every insurance dollar you spend and figure out if it provides any real benefit for you.

Interactive Activity: Find ways to Save Money

1. We can find many ways to save money. One of the easiest and most effective is to eliminate automatic billing of services that we no longer want. Do you have a subscription to a magazine or television channels that you don't want anymore? List 3 subscription services that you could cancel because you don't use them or don't want to use them anymore:

    1. _____

    2. _____

    3. _____

2. Another great place to save is to kick habits that waste money and that make our life worse. Have you been thinking about quitting cigarettes, alcohol or Starbucks? What about going out for lunch when it would be easier, quicker and cheaper to simply bring lunch to the office? List 3 things that you would like to remove from your life that use money:

1.

_____

2.

_____

3.

_____

3. List all the insurance services that you have. These include renter's, auto, home, medical, dental, vision, and pets.

_____

_____

_____

Now, go through each policy and delete all the stuff that you don't need.

SPENDING MONEY

Unless you are a hermit living in a cave in the mountains, you will spend money. We can use technology to spend less money that would would otherwise, and even get more of what we want and need in the process.

Comparison Sites

Before the Wealth Singularity began finding the best price was tricky. In fact, it was hit or miss. You traveled from store to store, checking prices (and wasting a lot of time and gas). Or, maybe your friend gave you the low down on a good price.

Now you can access online comparison sites and have a list of the best products at the best prices. Not only that, but will a cell phone you can check competing prices while you're already at a store.

Here are a few money-saving comparison sites:

- PriceGrabber
- Yahoo Shopping
- Deal Time
- Shopzilla
- Google Products
- Dealnews.com

Interactive Activity: Ways to Spend Money

1. When we have the urge to spend, it often passes after a short time. Find ways to disperse the desire by doing something that makes money or helps you. List 10 things that you could do (but only if you want to) instead of spending money. They can include exercise, connecting with others, or an idea from this book.

_____

_____

_____

_____

2. Get in the habit of comparison price shopping. Choose an item you were thinking about buying, and spend 15 minutes looking for the best price online. Check the above sites and bookmark the ones you like best.

3. Spend money on the important things. While it is important to stop spending on things that we don't need and don't serve us, it is equally important to spend money on the things that help us. They include activities that improve our health, learning programs that improve our life or our future earning power. List 3 things that you choose to continue spending money on because they serve you:

1.

_____

2.

_____

3.

_____

INVESTING

Technology is making investing in stocks, options, and other assets easier. But the Wealth Singularity will give you access to investing tools that were once thought unimaginable.

You'll be able to:

- Access information and indicators in real time.
- Utilize predictive models.
- Unleash computing power far beyond the power of just a few years ago.
- Tap into artificial intelligence and other forms of advanced technology.

And you can do it while you sleep, walk the dog, have dinner with your spouse, or while doing anything else.

This Wealth Singularity revolution is called Automated Trading and, sometimes, algorithmic trading.

But if you want to get ahead of this Wealth Singularity curve, you should learn more about Automated Trading and determine if it makes sense to utilize in your own investing practice.

We'll talk about how this aspect of the Wealth Singularity will change how you invest now.

Why Invest?

Investing is one of the most effective ways of building wealth. The main advantage of investing is that it allows us to use our existing money to create more money. And, this is done through by freeing ourselves from the wage slavery mindset.

When we work for money in an job at an hourly or annual wage, our income is limited to our time. Sure, it is possible to work overtime or even get a second job, but these measures are hardly a solution to creating wealth. When our income is determined by the time we put into a job, it will always be limited by the number of hours we can work the amount of effort that we can generate. Both of these are limited.

In contrast, when we invest, our income is not directly limited by time or effort. It is only limited by our investing skills, and the amount of money we have to invest. Fortunately for us, both of these quantities can be readily increased.

Investing is a skill, just like writing, or selling or driving a car. At first, we are quite clueless. It is natural to know nothing because the subject of investing is totally ignored in school. That means that we have to learn how to invest on our own time with our own effort, without anyone around us telling us that we have to do it. Through practice and learning, our investing expertise will improve and we will become skilled investors.

In addition, the amount of money that we have will naturally increase. As we become competent investors, we learn that money has significant value, *even if we don't spend it*. This is in clear contrast to the common consumer mindset that is dominates this country. The money that we invest grows and grows, only to become more money later. When we start out investing, we often have nothing to invest. However, it only takes a few years to create significant wealth through investing.

Automated Trading

Automated trading uses computers to automatically place trades for you. It's probably the best example of how the Wealth Singularity will change investing.

In Automated Trading. your trades can be based on technical or fundamental factors, or any other stock-picking practice. Alternatively, a famous trader can send out position calls based on his or her own calls or methodology.

The calls are enacted nearly instantaneously through Internet technology, so there's very little lag between when the call is made and when the actual transaction takes place.

Automated Trading and our Financial Future

If we created a time line of Automated Trading and compared it to a similar time line of, let's say, Internet technology, it's a good guess that we're probably in the late 1990s. The technology is almost there. The ideas are peculating. And the early adopters are already in the pool.

But problems arise with the adoption and distribution of the technology. In the early days of the Internet, only a few people with dial-up access could go online and few saw the ultimate value of the Internet. It wasn't until a few "killer apps" (like e-mail) arose that more chose to adopt online technology and reached its current stage of mass distribution.

Automated Trading is demonstrating a similar trajectory.

For instance, Automated Trading technology is being used by bigger investment firms. There isn't a trader pushing a button for each trade. More than likely, Automated Trading systems are making the day-to-day (or minute-to-minute) trades for most investment firms.

However, individual investors tend to be skeptical of Automated Trading. Even though most of their money is being managed, in part, by computers, they would never segment a portion of their self-managed portfolio to a machine.

But that will change.

Why the Wealth Singularity Supports Automated Trading

Automated Trading offers busy investors and traders a chance to reap the high returns of trading with the ease of automation. It's like having a high-return mutual fund. This isn't just for stocks. Automated trading can be used with any asset: stocks, commodities, and Forex. And, that could be just the beginning. There's no reason to suppose that Automated Trading couldn't be used for exotic trading and exotic derivatives, like credit and interest rate swaps.

Online Investing AI will take Automated Trading one step further. We're creating advanced Artificial Intelligence technologies that select strategies for asset trading. The technologies are designed to produce buy/sell/hold strategies that offer lower risk levels at higher return rates. We believe that this technology can trade other assets, like Forex, as well.

As with all residual income-producing systems, there are still pros and cons.

Pros
Automatic and automated means there's very little time to set up or maintain. Another benefit: for those who don't have the time to trade or research investments, Automated Trading has the potential to mimic the high

returns of trading without the time and research.

Cons
Poor systems do exist. One thing to watch: developers will create systems that work for a few months and quit. Automated Trading systems must be nimble to produce strategies that change with the market.

Resources:

- Online Investing AI
- Collective 2
- Strategy Exchange

Can Automated Trading Outperform Human Trading?

One classic argument is the man-versus-machine debate that's been going on, probably since the first time a wheel rolled out of a cave. And it reminds me of a story.

My friend was in one of those boring business meetings where a talking suit tells you how competitive the industry is. This speaker said the competition was circling like a lion around a herd of gazelles.

He then said, rhetorically, "If the industry is a gazelle, we have to be what?"

"Be the fastest gazelle," the speaker said, answering his own question.

My friend, who is pretty sharp, replied (as dozens of eyes fell on him), "That's not true. We just have to be faster than the slowest gazelle."

Everyone cracked up and even though it's funny, it brings up my point about Automated Trading systems. Can an Automated Trading system beat every human trader? Maybe not.

What I want it to do is beat *my* trading returns, though, right? And I think a properly developed Automated Trading system can do that. After all, it has several advantages. It doesn't stop. It doesn't sleep. It doesn't get bored of looking at charts and stock quotes. It doesn't take bathroom breaks or decide it would rather go jogging when it should be researching Forex patterns.

So, I think, I may not be the slowest gazelle on the trading floor, but I think there are Automated Trading systems that are a little bit faster and more reliable. If they're offering to carry my on their back, why not take a ride?

Trend Following

Automated Trading isn't the only way you can hook into the Wealth Singularity.

Some people, believe it or not, like to work to make money. They're called traders. They look at the market as a puzzle they want to solve, or look at it like it's a dragon to be slayed.

That doesn't mean you shouldn't use a guidebook to help you solve the puzzle, or use the best weapons to slay that dragon. For traders, computer technology can make trade methods, like Trend Following, easier.

Trend Following is nothing more than noticing long, definite price movements in assets and taking positions in those moves.

Of all the investment methods, Trend Following has one of the largest followings and a pretty solid track record.

The pioneer of trend following was Rich Dennis, a madcap investor from Chicago who turned a couple hundred bucks into a couple hundred million bucks by watching for well-defined trends. Instead of betting on each price movement, Dennis, and later his group of disciples called "The Turtles", looked for solid movements that were indicated by breakouts.

Even though this sounds relatively easy, the group of Turtles interviewed for the book, The Complete Turtle Trader, by Michael W. Covel, admitted that it could be, at turns, boring and stressful–two emotions that lead to investment mistakes.

In the book, Dennis adds that technology has made it easier for trend following:

"Given what the computer can do today–compared to what it could do a few years ago, I just can't see how any human could possibly compete with a well-designed computerized set of systems."

One of our partners, INO has developed several applications for technical analysis that would help trend following traders. You can use their free analysis to determine possible buy and sell points, for example. You'll have the report emailed to you. Other tools include a complete set of educational videos from professional traders.

You can add Automated Trading to your trend trading practice This lets the trader do things like sleep, let's say, or hang out with friends and have a family life.

Another advantage is, although technology can help the trader immensely, it can't edit out totally human emotions. Those emotions (like fear and greed) can cause traders to buy into a trend that is waning and avoiding a trade that is building.

Resources for Trend Following:

- Online Investing AI
- Online Investing AI Blog
- INO.com
- Trend Following by Michael Covel

Success Case 1: Paulson's Billions

According to the Wall Street Journal, hedge fund manager John Paulson noticed the housing price trends in the early 2000s had far out-paced historic trends.

He decided a new trend was coming--a massive drop in home prices. In the Wealth Singularity, smart traders can make money going up, or going down. Paulson made an astute bet that the prices would decline.

Then, he and his wife went on vacation.

During the vacation, Paulson's wife went to the ATM to check the balance. When she looked at the statement, she was more than a little surprised to see the figure: $45 million.

Over the next few months, the $45 million would be a drop in the bucket. The hedge fund manager was making about $10 million a day. His broker even had to remind him that he had a $5 million account still open.

Success Case 2: College Student Creates a Hedge Fund

Before the onset of the Wealth Singularity, you'd never have heard of a college student becoming a hedge fund manager. Most college students didn't even invest.

Timothy Sykes is a pioneer in the Wealth Singularity.

Timothy Sykes, author of the book, An American Hedge Fund, was born in Orange, Connecticut in 1981. He studied Philosophy and Business at Tulane University while turning his $12,415 Bar Mitzvah Gift money into a fully audited pre-tax sum of $1.65 million from 1999 to 2002 before founding his hedge fund, Cilantro Fund Management, LLC in 2003.

Investing Resources

There are more technological resources available for investors now than ever. Whether it's meeting fellow investors or previewing what other assets traders think about investments and assets, the number of social networks, web sites, blogs, and online tools seems to increasing each day.

Here are ten of the most popular stock trading social networks and social bookmarking sites that have investors and traders in mind.

- Tip'd (www.tipd.com)
  Tip'd is an investor's Digg. But it isn't just for investors and traders; its social link sharing service has lots of links to blog posts and articles about personal finance, real estate, innovation, and other business-related topics.

- Zecco (www.zecco.com)
  Zecco is a low-cost brokerage. But it's one of the first to recognize that trading is a social occupation. The brokerage built a community to share ideas and pass along insights.

- Stockpickr (www.stockpickr.com)
  Stockpickr doesn't just let you know what the average investor is thinking; you can see what moves other famous investors–like Warren Buffet–are making.

- MoneyVidya (www.moneyvidya.com)
  Trading and investing is a global business. MoneyVidya is an Indian stock-trading network.

- Stocktwits (www.stocktwits.com)
  Take twitter and add traders and you got Stocktwit. It's a fun approach to collective intelligence for traders.

- iStockAnalyst (www.istockanalyst.com)
  This site lets users read and submit articles about trades and investments.

- Trader Planet (www.traderplanet.com)
  Described as "a one stop shop for stock market beginners," Trader Planet also features a community and provides "news, research and training for professionals and seasoned expert."

- Tickerheads (www.tickerheads.com)
  Tickerheads is a community for trading ideas and social network for traders and investors.

- Feed the Bull (www.feedthebull.com)
  Feed the Bull is a social bookmarking service that allows people the opportunity to add links to articles and blog posts about investment and trading issues.

- Covestor (www.covestor.com)
  Covestor is part social network and part broker. You can post your stock picks and the site automatically tracks your performance. If you do well, people will begin to follow your trades and maybe even pay you for your guidance. Likewise, you can follow trading gurus and automatically make the same trades that they do.

Investing with Online Investing AI

One of the reasons that we are really excited about the Wealth Singularity is that it will improve the lives of people throughout the world. Just as Ford's assembly line brought the automobile into the reach of mainstream America, we believe that accelerating technology will radically help the billions of people on this planet.

This accelerating technology makes real software and services that were previously thought impossible. Creating systems to automatically buy and sell stocks that consistently make money was once thought to be impossible, many people still believe that it is. However, accelerating technology is changing that.

As computers get faster and faster, we are able to use them to solve previously impossible problems. Another force that is helping is the advancement of artificial intelligence. New software and algorithms allow us to create systems that are more reliable and more profitable.

One of the goals of our company, Online Investing AI, is to help people throughout the world use accelerating technology to make money. The best way that we have found to make this happen is through the use of Automated Trading systems. We believe that as technology improves, it will become easier and safer to generate income through these systems.

We are developing the technology to achieve these goals. Here are some screenshots of the beta version of the software.

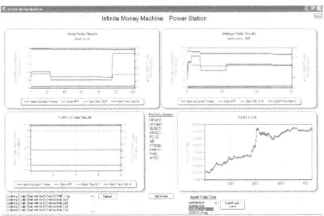

Our systems are developed by using a variety of Artificial Intelligence technologies to overcome the traditional limitations of trading systems. We use neural nets, Genetic Algorithms, and fuzzy logic to create these new Automated Trading systems.

We are still in the technical development process, and therefore have not yet released our systems. We feel that it is critical to create something that is going to work and create value for our clients. To find out the latest developments for both the software and the company, be sure to check our blog.

Interactive Activity: Ways to Invest Money

1. Take a moment to consider the various investing vehicles that you have learned. Which ones are you naturally attracted to? Which ones are you interested in? Which do you think you would be good at or would like to invest a little effort to learn more about? List 5 below:

   1.

   _____

   2.

   _____

   3.

   _____

   4.

   _____

   5.

   _____

2. Out of the 5 above, choose 3 to do more research on. Check the web sites that we have mentioned, or consider getting a book or other resource on the subject. Write the 3 down below and spend 10 minutes learning more about each one. Take notes below and create bookmarks so you can continue your learning later.

_____

_____

_____

_____

3. Set a one-year goal. How much passive income from your investments are you interested in making? Set a goal to make the following amount of money per month, starting 12 months from now. This goal is far enough so that you can assemble the resources to achieve it, and close enough to keep you focused. Write the goal here:

_____

_____

_____

_____

ADJUST YOUR MINDSET

Although this is a book about technology and wealth, it would not be complete without a few words about our own mind. Everything that we create in this world (including technology, business and money) is a result of our thinking. If our thinking is bankrupt, our wallets will surely follow. If our thinking is dominated by reasons why investing won't work, then we will never try.

We need to spend just as much effort working on our minds as we do on our finances. Most people spend all their energy on their job, and have nothing left over for themselves. This is the mental equivalent of spending all our income before the month is over.

Instead, I suggest that we spend time each day working on our mind, on improving ourselves. It could be through reading a book, listening to a CD set, or just working on a money-making idea while taking a walk.

This book is full of resources that you can use to improve your mind. Take a moment to figure out what is best for you. We don't have to read a book if we hate reading. If you like listening to an interesting speaker, get a CD set. Or, if you prefer interactive learning, sign up for a seminar. It doesn't matter which way we choose to improve ourselves. It only matters that we choose to do it, and find a way that works for us.

Goal Setting

Part of setting up our minds for success in knowing exactly where we are going to go in life. Most people just drift along with the flow of society. They go to school as they are told. Then they get a job. Then they get married, get a mortgage, and have kids. They go through their whole life without ever deciding what they really want.

Instead of just doing things because everyone else is doing them, we suggest taking the time to think out what we would like our destination to be. Most people choose a major or get a job because of some proficiency that they have developed. They say, "I was always good with computers, so I became a programmer." Don't do this! It is a recipe for mediocrity and dissatisfaction.

We think it might be a good idea to really think about what we want to do, instead of what we are good at. Are you more interested in marketing that computer programming? Do you enjoy connecting with people more than monkeying around with spreadsheets? Any skill can be developed over time, and the tools to learn anything are more available than ever.

The concept of goal setting does not apply only to our job or career. It applies to every aspect of our lives. This includes finances, friends, relationships, travel, cars, houses, spirituality, fun, our body, health, and happiness.

The human mind is the most powerful

computer in existence (at least for now!). And it is also a goal-seeking machine. When we give it precise targets, it naturally directs itself to hit them. If we don't *consciously* set our targets, then other people and other forces around us will set them for us. We need to set them ourselves so we go where we want to go.

So, take a moment and write down your top 5 goals: These can include the areas of:

- money
- career
- environment (house, cars, location, etc.)
- relationships
- spirituality
- body and health

Interactive Activity: Create a Brighter Future

1. What *could* you do to improve my mind? What resources *could* you buy or borrow that could improve your financial future?

List 10 items that could improve your financial future:

1.
_____

2.
_____

3.
_____

4.
_____

5.
_____

6.
_____

7.
_____

8.
_____

9.
_____

10.

_____

2. Out of the list above, what *one item* are you willing to get or do right now? If possible, order the item online right now. Write that item here:

_____

3. What can you change about your daily routine to improve your mind? Could you listen to learning CDs while in the car? Can you put some helpful information in your iPod so you can listen to it while you work out? Can you read a book when you wake up or before you go to sleep?

List 5 ways you can improve your daily routine:

1.

_____

2.

_____

3.

_____

4.

_____

5.

_____

Resources - Taking the Next Step

Would you like to learn more about developing your mind into a machine that will help you achieve your goals? The above activities are a great first step. Here are some other resources that we have found useful:

Books

- Rich Dad, Poor Dad by Robert Kiyosaki
- Conspiracy of the Rich by Robert Kiyosaki
- Secrets of the Millionaire Mind by T. Harv Eker

CD Sets

- Get the Edge by Tony Robbins

Becoming a Wealth Generator Instead of a Wage Earner

There are two prevalent mind sets in the work world. You are either a wage-earner or a wealth generator. There are advantages--and disadvantages--to both, but these mindsets are critical in how you experience wealth.

How you arrived at your mindset is complex. The way your family and friends approach wealth has an effect on whether you consider yourself a wealth-generator or a wage earner. Your own explorations and inclinations are other causes. But, there is no doubt that the social forces tend to push you into the wage-earner mindset.

There are three social forces that advocate the wage-earner mindset.

Schools
Our educational system is set up to train wage earners.

If you ask teachers what the goal of the good education they provide, a majority will tell you they hope their students get good jobs.

They almost never say they hope their students create wealth. In fact, wealth is somewhat of a bad word in state educational systems.

Another way that schools prepare us to be wage earners is through its division of reward system. Wage earners are given tasks that they perform and then are reviewed on that performance by a boss or manager. Rarely are workers asked to apply the lessons learned from their tasks to generate wealth with other ideas. Likewise students are given tasks and rewarded on those tasks by teachers.

Those tasks, in and of themselves, aren't bad things, but they don't teach a holistic approach, or seek to invigorate innovation.

Work

The workplace is really just an extension of the school system. Most people send their children to school without thinking about it, and without giving their children a choice. The children graduate from school, and assume that their next obligatory routine is to get a job. Work gives people a place to go everyday when they are done with school.

It's hard to tell our schools are based on our workplaces, or our workplaces are based on our schools, but the similarities between the two can not be denied.

The workplace is structured in a top-down approach. It all starts with a CEO. In schools, superintendents and principals would fill that position. CEOs delegate their power to managers and then to supervisors. Likewise, principals pass on their power to teachers and then to certain students.

You can trace both organizations back to mass production factory floors, the earliest real example of organizational science in the United States.

What served us well in the 18th century is woefully unable to keep up with the rapidly-evolving technology. New types of technology are used to bolster the current structure instead of exploring new avenues to productivity.

The organization most workers experience

today is rigid and slow. Workers are willing to exchange their individuality and innovative ability for a steady paycheck and security.

This has created a wage-slavery mentality. When you exchange your time for money, you'll never come out ahead. True wealth extends beyond time. Creating a product idea, for example, may only take an instant and, yet, it can produce a stream of income perpetually. Likewise, a blog post that took a few minutes to write can produce money through advertising and affiliate sales as long as you'll host the article.

This isn't a new concept to the owners of factories and businesses. They've realized for years (or centuries) that passing on money for people's time was a great deal, so long as they were keeping a portion of the income from their ideas.

Prior to the dawning of the Wealth Singularity, workers had little options. Raising the capital necessary to build a factory was a considerable barrier to entry. Now, however, you have more computing power resting in the computer on your lap than NASA had during the manned moon mission. In an age where ideas will dominate, this computing power is the key to your future wealth.

And your independence.

The Government
It's not the job of the government to solve problems; the government must sustain

problems and create new problems.

Why?

If it solved a problem, why would we need a government? Why would we need government workers? And why would we need politicians and their minions?

As proof, is it any coincidence that most major government programs have not ended due to successfully ending the problem it was charged to stop? After trillions of dollars, has the War on Poverty ended poverty? Have the billions spent on schools made students smarter?

Actually, the problems grow--and with it the government infrastructure needed to sustain it (and government jobs). Social Security started out as essentially a stipend for the old and widows and children. It now includes disability (some of which are questionable disabilities). It's not a stipend; some Americans look on it as their only retirement plan.

Whether it's intentional or not, the tax structure keeps people dependent. The more income taxpayers make, the more they pay. Taxes on investment border on confiscatory. Dividends are taxed twice: when the company makes the profit and when the investor receives the dividend (as income). If the investor reinvests dividends, he or she could be taxed without ever seeing a penny of income.

Critics of the tax system say that this tax on

investing--and the lack of taxes on spending and credit use--has created a nation of spenders, not savers.

How Do You Break Free?

With schools, your boss, and the government conspiring to keep you poor, how do you break free?

The first step is to recognize that these obstacles exist. Whether they are intentional, or an accident of social order, hardly matters. It would be like a slave who sees that the fence is open deciding he won't try to escape unless he finds out exactly what socio-economic forces were involved in the creation of slave labor.

Get free first. Ask questions later.

Once you do recognize the limitations of the work-for-a-living world, you're next step is to develop the proper mindset that will lead you into the Wealth Singularity. It's something you can work on at your own pace. There's no need to quit your job and live in a cave. You'll soon realize that the cubicle walls are flimsy compared to the mental barriers you set for yourself.

In the next section, we'll lead you to the ultimate Wealth Singularity.

The one in your mind.

Mind Tools for the Wealth Singularity

Visualization

Visualization can help you enter the Wealth Singularity. Visualization is a form of mental rehearsal, but many believe it's much more powerful than that. Some believe, just like software, visualization is a form of commands for the universe. Once you master the symbolic language of it, it can produce any result you want.

Whether you believe there's a mystical connection between the universe and your vision, or you believe that visualization is just good preparation, the success of mental rehearsal has been proven.

It can help you create wealth-generating ideas.

It can improve your trading and investing skills. It can even help you save money.

There's actually nothing that mental rehearsal can't help you achieve.

To make visualization more effective, here are a few tips.

Pick Your Perspective

Experts seem to be divided into two camps on this one. Some experts say to make the visualization first-hand; in other words, you are actually looking out from yourself and seeing the task being accomplished. Another school of thought says to visualize in the third-person; you are watching yourself take part in the activities, or accomplishing the goal. Try both and determine which one feels better and, of course, which one achieves the best results.

Feel It

For visualization to be successful, experts say you shouldn't just visualize it, you should feel it real. Use all of your senses: hearing, seeing, touching, smelling, and even tasting.

Follow The Process

A new theory is that visualization is more successful when you visualize the entire process. Don't just visualize your income statement going up, see the trading opportunities arise, see the numbers, see the chart, see yourself making the trade, then see the income statement. Go through the whole process.

Practice

Make visualization an actual practice. Don't just resort to it in times of need. When you approach it in only in desperation, visualization tends to be another type of meditation: worry. It's better to find a corner in your busy day, relax, keep silent, and engage in your visualization exercises.

Meditation

"Empty your mind, be formless, shapeless - like water. Now you put water into a cup, it becomes the cup, you put water into a bottle, it becomes the bottle, you put it in a teapot, it becomes the teapot. Now water can flow or it can crash. Be water, my friend."

-- Bruce Lee

No matter how much money you have and no matter how well you've mastered the wealth-making technologies and systems we've discussed in this book, you will not progress into the Wealth Singularity unless you can master your mind.

The mind is your greatest ally or worst enemy.

It explains why there are unhappy rich people and ecstatically happy poor people.

The study of meditation is an ancient art based on the notion that the mind can make a heaven of hell, or a hell of heaven. Meditation is a process of quieting the mind. At the most esoteric level, experts in meditation say that a quiet mind taps into the deepest levels of consciousness, a level that is at the root of one's being.

Other practitioners aren't as philosophical; they are more utilitarian. Meditation, they say, is calming. By quieting the mind, the repetitive, anxious thoughts can be cleared.

There are hundreds of meditation techniques

and technology. Here are a few you can experiment with.

Following your Breath

One of the easiest meditation techniques is the breath-following meditation.

Find a quiet spot, a place you won't be easily distracted or interrupted.

Sit down in a comfortable position. Most people tend to sit cross-legged or in a lotus position with feet folded onto the thighs, but neither is necessary. You just don't want to get too comfortable; you may fall asleep. (Don't fret if that happens either.)

While sitting, begin to focus on your breaths. Follow your inhale into your chest; watch your exhale leave your body. When other thoughts and worries come, let them in and release them. Then, return to watching your breath.

There's no set time limit for this meditation. Even five minutes spent in a deeply-relaxed breath-following meditation will calm you down and focus you mind.

It's also a great meditation to do during work, before you need to focus on a task or are trying to solve a challenge.

Watching your Thoughts

Watching your thoughts is similar to breath-following.

You can even combine the two.

Start in a seated position and relax. Take a few deep breaths and let them out in long, slow exhalations.

You'll immediately begin to recognize your thoughts. Instead of resisting them, go with them. Most particularly examine the silent spaces between the thoughts. You have identified with your thoughts for so long, this silent space should be a mystery. If you are not just your thoughts, what is this silent space between your thoughts? Who is this?

You can set a timer and watch your thoughts for as long as you like.

Mantra

A mantra is a word that focuses your mind. Some meditation schools believe that you need a special word that is given to you by a guru. But, according to one story, a group of meditation teachers made their students focus on the word ba-na-na--with similar effect.

Just like breath-watching and thought-watching, you should watch your mantra, which ever one you have selected. Intone the word slowly and consciously. There are mixed opinions on whether the mantra should be spoken out loud, or if it can be silently pronounced. The best advice is to try both and select the one that both fits your life and has the most success.

Zen

Zen meditation uses the breath-watching technique, or utilizes a concentration technique where practitioners focus their attention on a space below their navels to attain a oneness with reality--called samadhi.

While you might not receive enlightenment from your zen practice, beginning zen students report that the meditation is calming and improves concentration. Scientific studies bear this out.

According to a study from Emory University School of Medicine, people who practice zen meditation–sometimes called zazen–can edit out distractions better than folks who don't meditate.

Researchers examined blood flow in the brain when the subjects were interrupted by stimuli that was meant to imitate distracting thoughts. Meditators can deal with the interruption and return to the task at hand.

This study also suggest that meditation can help people manage distracting thoughts.

Improved productivity would be one benefit and a limit of obsessive negative thinking would be another.

Yoga

Yoga is a pretty popular activity now. But, the yoga that you see, typically during commercials for health food, where beautiful people are stretching out in and gazing serenely into a sunrise is only one type of the ancient art of yoga.

Here are other branches of yoga:

- Bhakti yoga -- spiritual devotion
- jnana yoga -- rational inquiry
- raja yoga -- concentration
- karma yoga -- path of right action

The type you're most familiar with is called hatha yoga and it's goal is to unite the physical with the spiritual through a series of strength and flexibility exercises. A yoga routine can vary from minutes to hours, but a 15-minute session each day is perfect for mind-balancing session.

You can check out these sites to learn more about how to incorporate yoga into your mindset-adjusting practice:

- Yoga Journal
- About.com's Yoga site
- Yoga Basics

Brain Technology

Technology is creating faster, smarter, and more powerful machines. But some futurists speculate that the two paths of intelligence-- human and machine--will fuse.

A good example of this is the new brain technology that's being developed. Many users already report that the technology that is currently on the market is already beneficial and future versions are even more powerful.

The brain technology currently available includes paraliminals, subliminals, binaural beats, and biofeedback.

Paraliminal and subliminal technology are based on the theory that super fast messages can bypass the conscious mind and seep the information directly into your subconscious. Binaural beats synch up brainwaves with specific wave patterns, allowing you to reach an optimal mindset. Biofeedback relies on bio-indicators, like pulse and blood pressure, to achieve an improved state of mind.

From our own investigation, we've found that half the people claim the technology has helped them, while half the people say that the technology hasn't. However, just as technology will drive innovation in other areas of life, it will make even more powerful mind-optimizing technology.

You can investigate and experiment with technology at the following sites:

- EOC Institute
- Binaural Beats
- Learning Strategies--Paraliminals
- Real Subliminal
- Pick The Brain

Creating a Visualization, Meditation Practice

We mentioned that your should create a meditation or visualization practice. How do you do that? You're so busy, right? To meditate you need to have a cave, or at least access to a monastery.

That's what a lot of people think, but actually, you can start a practice with a few minutes a day, anywhere you want. Here are a few tips:

Are you a morning person or night owl? Your first step in creating a practice is to determine when you feel like your mind is at its peak. Most people are either morning or night people. Although, some people are lunch people and some are mid-afternoon people! It doesn't matter. If you feel better in the morning, carve out some time for meditation then. If you like to stay up late, make time to meditate then.

Once you get into this more, you might have two meditation sessions. Maybe a visualization period in the morning to get you revved up and meditation in the evening to calm your mind.

Set a time limit
The time you spend meditating is, initially, less important than your consistency and commitment. Once you carve out the time in your schedule, you can slowly build the amount of time you spend meditating and visualizing.

For instance, you can begin with a five-minute session. In a week, add another five minutes. A week later, add one more five-minute session and so on, until you reach the level you want.

Find a space
Eliminate distractions by finding a quiet, low-trafficked space in your home or apartment. Clear out the area and add decorations that make you feel calm--art work, statues, objects, etc.

Using the same space can underline the commitment you have in your routine.

Once you enter, you should almost feel a sense of calmness.

Get in the mood
Play music or read passages and scriptures that inspire you or make you feel meditative.

This will help your brain start to sink into those depths of thought.

Start the habit
Meditating each day is a great habit to start.

In the next section, we'll give you tips on how to create positive habits.

The Power of Habit

The weight of the chains of habit are too light to be felt...until they are too heavy to be thrown off.

Once we have created a mindset that serves us, there is one more piece that we need to achieve our goals: action. No matter how well we think, our achievement in life will ultimately be determined by how effectively we turn our thoughts into results. Here's one powerful strategy to make our successful mindset work for us, and at the same time require a minimum of effort.

Habits are one of the most powerful and least noticed forces in our lives. These are thousands of tiny actions that we do each day without even thinking about them. Habits are the automatic pilot that make life quite easy for our conscious minds. Yet, habits that harm us are incredibly difficult to get rid of.

If we didn't have habits, we could never get though our day. Before we took any action, we would have to think about endless ramifications of our every action. Do you automatically brush your teeth at the beginning or end of the day? With the *habit* of brushing our teeth, we would have to think about why, when and how we should brush our teeth. However, since it is a habit, it happens automatically and we don't even need to think about it.

Brushing our teeth is a habit that serves us. It keeps our mouth clean, massages our gums and prevents cavities. We are better off because we have this simple habit. In contrast, we also have habits that do not help us. In fact, they hurt us. Do you (or anyone you know) have any of these habits?

- smoking
- drinking too much
- eating too much
- eating junk food
- spending too much
- treating people harshly

This list could go on for pages, but you get the idea! These habits, or addictions, are simply patterns of action that we have fallen into. These actions, unlike brushing our teeth, make our lives and our futures worse, and therefore they harm us.

The interesting thing about habits is that they are quite easy to create, but hard to change once they are created. Almost everyone has identified habits that they want to get rid of. We won't mention the useless and ubiquitous advice to just stop these habits. However, here are some ways of using habits to serve us.

Although it is difficult to stop a habit, it is quite easy to change them. If I were addicted to overeating, I would replace the unhealthy food with salad. I could still get the satisfaction of a full stomach, but can also escape the negative health effects of potato chips and Big Macs. Another example is for people who smoke. It is fairly easy to replace smoking a cigarette with another habit, such as chewing gum.

Most people go through their entire lives never taking control of their habits. And, as we have seen, habits are one of the most powerful determinants of our destination in life. Now we are going to stop and think about some positive habits that we can create. Once we install positive habits into our daily routine, it makes it easy to benefit automatically without having to go through the rigmarole of deciding to do it.

Here is a short list of positive habits that you might want to have:

- Daily walking, running or other exercise
- Writing in journal
- Noticing what we are grateful for
- Writing down everything we did to improve our future today
- Reading a book or other resource about self improvement
- Investing 30 minutes to achieve financial freedom

These are just a few ideas off the top of my head, and I am sure you can think of some of your own. Now it's your turn.

Interactive Activity: Create a Habit that Serves You

1. Make a list of 10 habits that *could* serve you. (But you do not have to do them unless you want to!) They could improve any aspect of your life, including your health, relationships, finances, environment, or anything else. This is a brainstorming exercise, so just write down whatever comes to mind!

1. _____

2. _____

3. _____

4. _____

5. _____

6. _____

7. _____

8.

_____

9.

_____

10.

_____

2. Choose 1 new habit that you might be willing to create. It should be simple, easy to understand, and doable on a daily basis. Write down that habit. Now, write down 5 benefits that you would get from that new habit. These could include "improve my health", "make me feel great", or "improve my finances".

My new habit is

_____

The 5 benefits I get from my new habit are:

1.

_____

2.

_____

3.

_____

4.

_____

5.

_____

3. Decide if you are willing to adopt this new habit starting right now. If you are, great! If not, redesign the habit so that you are willing to do it on a daily basis. Change it so that it fits in with what you are willing to commit to. Now, write down the new habit that you are committed to doing on a daily basis here:

_____

One key to developing a new habit is that you *do it every day*. That means every day. Not only when we feel like it. Not only when the weather is good. They must be done *every single day*. Why? Because, otherwise, they do not develop into powerful habits and we lose the benefit.

The easiest and most effective way to install a habit is to do it every day at the same time. I suggest to do it in the morning, and wake up early to do it. If it takes 30 minutes, then wake up 30 minutes early. However, each person is different. You can do it during your commute, when you come home from work, or in the evening before bed. It doesn't matter when you do it, just that you find a time that works for you on a daily basis.

If you find a time for the habit and it gets done every day, then it only takes about 3 weeks to become a habit. Instead of having to push yourself to do the activity, the habit will push you to do it. Similarly to brushing our teeth, the new habit will become part of our everyday schedule and happen automatically.

CONCLUSION

The human race is on the edge of a brand new age of existence. Consider the life of the first human beings that had the same genetic makeup as us, who walked the earth 100,000 years ago. They woke up each day, hunted animals and collected fruits, and returned to their cave to sleep until the next day.

Not much changed during their entire lives. They had the same language, the same tools, the same weapons. Nothing changed for thousands and thousands of years. It's hard for us to imagine what such a life could be like.

Now technology changes on an annual, if not monthly basis. What was an expensive luxury a few years ago is now cheap and commonplace. This is the magic of technological advancement and improvement. It works hand in hand with efficient market and distribution systems.

The interesting aspect of this dramatic revolution is that the *rate of change* is accelerating. As technology and everything else around us changes, it causes all the other changes and improvements to accelerate.

This singular time in human history, and perhaps in the history of the universe, offers incredible and unique benefits for those of us who use it. We can be slaves to society and technology, or we can be rulers. We can use the power and leverage of accelerating technology to our advantage, and overcome all of the barriers and problems that hold us back.

Although this book is largely about how to improve our finances, it is also about how to improve every aspect of our lives. Technology can be used to make friends just as easily as it is used to make money. It can be used to make ourselves healthier, help others and to even control our own mind. The benefits are unlimited. The question is, how will we use technology to improve our life and the lives of others?

The last, and perhaps most important issue of note, is that these ideas will not do us any good if we leave them to merely percolate inside of our minds. Nothing happens until we take action, and now is the time to do it. Now that you have finished this book and are feeling motivated, choose to do the activities that are not yet finished.

Each step leads to the next. Action generates ideas, and ideas more action. The critical ingredient to success is to take the next step, no matter how small or trivial. It is the consistent footsteps of progress that make anything possible.

About Us

This book has been written by Matt and George. We also created of Online Investing AI web site and are developing the Infinite Money Machine. Our goal is to use technology to help everyone in the world succeed financially.

 Matt Swayne is a communications and marketing professional with more than 18 years experience. Matt currently works as a public relations and corporate communications specialist from one of the world's largest providers of online education. He is also an avid writer and blogger, who has worked with Startup Nation and Playboy Online. No stranger to startups, Matt has been a partner in and consultant to several startups.

 George Ulmer is a dancer. When he is not busy with what's really important, he is working on the Infinite Money Machine. He loves reading his favorite books, which are The Alchemist and Rich Dad Poor Dad. In a previous life, he was a computer programmer and built web sites. His favorite languages are French, Korean and Japanese.

What do you Think?

We value your opinion and feedback! Email us with your ideas and comments!

Email us!

- Matt@OnlineInvestingAI.com (the smart one)
- George@OnlineInvestingAI.com (the stupid one)

For the latest information, visit www.OnlineInvestingAI.com

www.ingramcontent.com/pod-product-compliance
Lightning Source LLC
Chambersburg PA
CBHW052148070326
40689CB00050B/2514